Hidden Depths

Amazing Underwater Discoveries

Written and illustrated by
TINA HOLDCROFT

Annick Press Ltd.
Toronto • New York • Vancouver

We acknowledge the support of the Canada Council for the Arts, the Ontario Arts Council, the Government of Ontario through the Ontario Book Publishers Tax Credit program and the Ontario Book Initiative, and the Government of Canada through the Book Publishing Industry Development Program (BPIDP) for our publishing activities.

Cataloging in Publication

Holdcroft, Tina
    Hidden depths : amazing underwater discoveries / Tina Holdcroft.

(Hidden! (Toronto, Ont.))
Includes bibliographical references and index.
ISBN 1-55037-863-5 (bound).—ISBN 1-55037-862-7 (pbk.)

    1. Shipwrecks—Juvenile literature. 2. Marine accidents—Juvenile literature. 3. Ocean—Juvenile literature. I. Title. II. Series.

G525.H75 2004   j910.4'52   C2004-902516-3

The art in this book was rendered in watercolor.
The text was typeset in Clearface, Officina, and Smile.

Distributed in Canada by:
Firefly Books Ltd.
66 Leek Crescent
Richmond Hill, ON
L4B 1H1

Published in the U.S.A. by Annick Press (U.S.) Ltd.
Distributed in the U.S.A. by:
Firefly Books (U.S.) Inc.
P.O. Box 1338
Ellicott Station
Buffalo, NY 14205

Manufactured in China.

Visit us at: www.annickpress.com

For Keith R. Morgan.
A sailor.
        —T.H.

Contents

Introduction

Ahoy thar mateys! Get out of your bathtubs and abandon the hunt for those deep-diving rubber duckies, those slippery bars of soap, those cheap plastic fish. Search instead through the pages of this book (dry your hands first) and see what's hiding under the wet stuff that covers over two-thirds of the planet.

Sink into some super stories of shipwrecks, a Civil War submarine, and a wicked sunken city. Take another breath, then dive down for a look at a long-lost lighthouse, a missing spacecraft, and a fish that everyone thinks is extinct.

There's much more to see beneath the sea. After all, it's the easiest place to lose things, the hardest place to search, and—from the shallow shores to the deep ocean bottom—it's the best hiding spot on earth!

Treasure Hunt

Gold, silver, jewels: fabulous riches hide under the sea, from shipwrecked treasure to seashell pearls.

What are you waiting for? Join the hunt and find a fortune!

START
Get ready to be amazed!

Feeling lucky?
Find a perfectly round pearl inside an oyster—but be prepared to open 10,000 shells to get one! In the 1900s, Japanese pearl farmers increase the odds by placing a round bead inside each oyster. The irritated shellfish coats the annoying object with nacre (pearly stuff) and spins a perfect underwater treasure.

Dine in style with 48,000 ceramic pieces found in the 1690 Chinese shipwreck VUNG TAO. Hidden under the sea near South Vietnam, these mostly blue-and-white porcelain treasures are dried off after a 301-year soak in the big sink. The undamaged pieces (28,000) are sold at auction in 1992 for $7.2 million U.S.

Your turn to do the dishes.

Hunt for a ship full of gold. In 1857, the SS CENTRAL AMERICA sank in the Atlantic near the U.S.A.'s Carolina coast while delivering three tons of California gold to New York City. In 1987, treasure hunters discover the deep wreck. Two years later, thousands of perfect, rare gold coins, nuggets, and bars are recovered. The treasure is worth over $100 million.

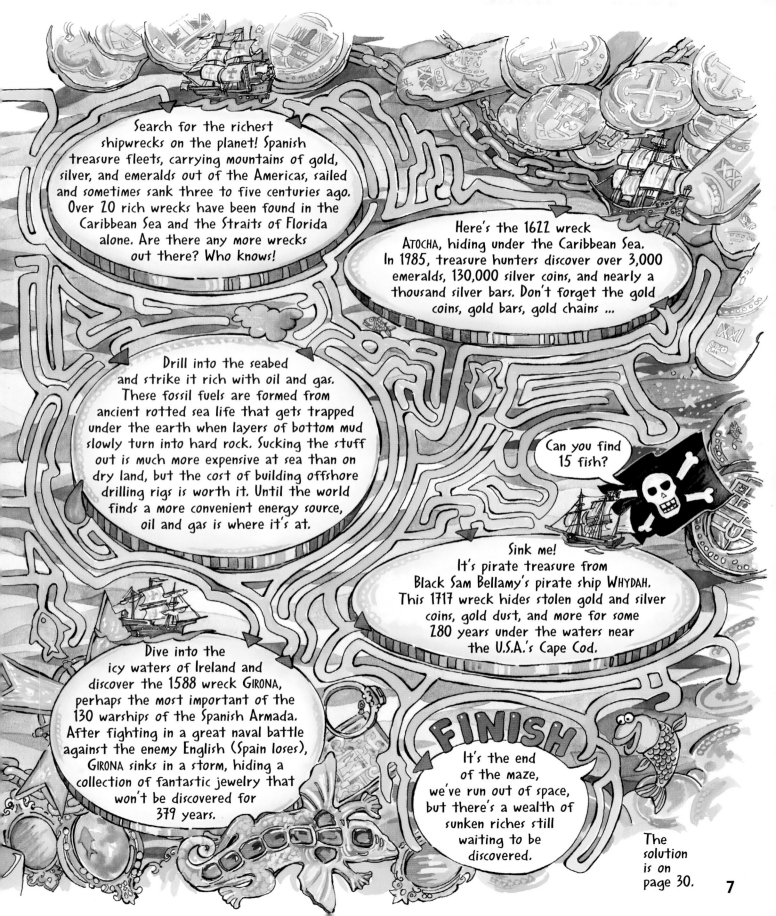

Search for the richest shipwrecks on the planet! Spanish treasure fleets, carrying mountains of gold, silver, and emeralds out of the Americas, sailed and sometimes sank three to five centuries ago. Over 20 rich wrecks have been found in the Caribbean Sea and the Straits of Florida alone. Are there any more wrecks out there? Who knows!

Here's the 1622 wreck ATOCHA, hiding under the Caribbean Sea. In 1985, treasure hunters discover over 3,000 emeralds, 130,000 silver coins, and nearly a thousand silver bars. Don't forget the gold coins, gold bars, gold chains ...

Drill into the seabed and strike it rich with oil and gas. These fossil fuels are formed from ancient rotted sea life that gets trapped under the earth when layers of bottom mud slowly turn into hard rock. Sucking the stuff out is much more expensive at sea than on dry land, but the cost of building offshore drilling rigs is worth it. Until the world finds a more convenient energy source, oil and gas is where it's at.

Can you find 15 fish?

Sink me! It's pirate treasure from Black Sam Bellamy's pirate ship WHYDAH. This 1717 wreck hides stolen gold and silver coins, gold dust, and more for some 280 years under the waters near the U.S.A.'s Cape Cod.

Dive into the icy waters of Ireland and discover the 1588 wreck GIRONA, perhaps the most important of the 130 warships of the Spanish Armada. After fighting in a great naval battle against the enemy English (Spain loses), GIRONA sinks in a storm, hiding a collection of fantastic jewelry that won't be discovered for 379 years.

FINISH

It's the end of the maze, we've run out of space, but there's a wealth of sunken riches still waiting to be discovered.

The solution is on page 30.

7

Ancient Sea Creatures

Is this a mistake? There's no water here, not even a puddle to paddle in! So what underwater thing can possibly hide on a mountain ridge nearly 2,500 meters (8,000 feet) high in the Canadian Rockies?

The answer hides inside this patch of soft shale rocks called the Burgess Shale. Split a rock and you'll find rare fossils of some of the earth's earliest and strangest creatures, from a time when this mountain ridge was under the edge of an ancient sea.

Scientists worldwide are amazed at this fantastic look at ancient animals and how they lived. They now have new clues to understanding the history of the earth.

Curious? Dip your toes into the waters of the past, but keep clear of that five-eyed thingy with the vacuum cleaner hose-nose!

This slab of shale is sea-bottom mud or sediment that's turned rock hard after millions of years. What's hiding in this sedimentary rock? It's easy to split, so let's take a look. Ah, a knobby-headed, pointy-tailed critter.

It's a beastie blast! For about 2 billion years, boring single-celled organisms are the only life form on the planet. But around 545 million years ago, a swarm of interesting multi-celled sea creatures suddenly burst on the scene. The Burgess Shale creatures lived in the sea only 40 million years after this creative creature explosion. In earth time, that's the blink of an eye.

Habelia

Hallucigenia

I'm old! Dinosaurs won't appear on earth for another 263 million years.

The earth's crust will shift quite a bit over the next half a billion years. Our seashore will be squashed between two pushy crustal plates and get shoved up out of the way.

Wow! How will our seashore end up in the mountains?

Odontogriphus

Long-lost Lighthouse

Sail back to the ancient past and steer for the bright beacon of the most famous lighthouse in history.

Built around 285 BCE, this towering landmark, called Pharos, will guide your ship past the dangerous sandbars under the Mediterranean Sea to the harbor of Egypt's great city, Alexandria.

You'll definitely want to write home about seeing this brilliant lighthouse. By day its giant mirror reflects the sun's rays, and by night a fire burns at the top of its tower, some 120 meters (400 feet) high.

Pharos is the tallest building on earth (except for two pyramids) and known as the seventh wonder of the ancient world!

But make sure to pick up a souvenir, like a Pharos-shaped lamp or a Roman coin with the lighthouse stamped right on it, because in 1303 a really bad earthquake topples the tower into the sea. That's the end of that!

Fort Qait Bey is built over the ruins in 1480 and a piece of the past is gone forever.

Forever? Never! Look what's hiding beneath the sea.

Some of these sculptured stones are hundreds of years older than the lighthouse.

You know what they say! Remove. Reuse. Redecorate.

In the early 1960s, amateur diver Kamel Abul Saadat discovers a jumble of building blocks, broken columns, statues, and sphinxes under Alexandria's seacoast. The Egyptian government pulls up a colossal statue and calls in archaeologist Honor Frost, who plunges into the project in 1968.

Hey, who's ruining the ruins? A 1990s harbor improvement plan calls for a new breakwater. A barge is dropping huge U-shaped concrete blocks into the sea, right on top of Pharos's sculpted stones. Crunch!

Lucky sphinx: it's the only sculpture that hasn't lost its head!

Around 2,000 years ago, the ancient traveler has a "must see" list of fantastic man-made objects called the Seven Wonders of the World. Today, only the first wonder still stands—Khufu's Great Pyramid of Giza in Egypt. (The other pyramids aren't on the list.)

Alexander the Great marches into Egypt in 331 BCE and starts a super-city at the western edge of the mouth of the river Nile. Under a series of Greek rulers, Alexandria soon brims with rich palaces, an awesome library, and a wonder of a lighthouse.

Darned earthquakes! From 320 to 1303 CE, Alexandria's coast gets shocked and rocked. Pharos and many shore-side buildings slide into the sea, including the palace that once belonged to Egypt's famous queen Cleopatra.

Pharos island gives its name to the lighthouse built on top. Today, all lighthouses in Italy and Spain are "faros," in France "phares."

Pharos had a gigantic door. This piece of door frame is taller than two giraffes.

Which reminds me, should phone Mother.

Compare this piece of statue with me. It's colossal!

It's a rescue mission! On October 4, 1995, archaeologist Jean-Yves Empereur gets the block-dropping barge to help pull 34 ancient wonders out of the sea.

The world is amazed—and so is the Egyptian government. They stop dropping concrete blocks over Pharos's stones, and Alexandria's underwater ruins become a protected archaeological zone.

Over 3,000 stone blocks blanket the seabed.

Wobbly Warship

How embarrassing! Everyone has come to the harbor at Stockholm, Sweden, to see *Vasa*, the most beautiful and mightiest warship of its day. It's August 10, 1628, and King Gustavus Adolphus's new ship, decorated with over 500 colorful woodcarvings, blasts her cannons to celebrate the beginning of her maiden voyage.

But Sweden's royal warship sails less than one and a half kilometers (one mile). Suddenly, the wind blows stronger and, in plain sight of everyone ashore, *Vasa* leans over and sinks!

After the last red-faced official stops shouting "It's your fault," *Vasa*'s shaky story starts to fade from memory. But the sunken ship seems determined to get a second chance to amaze the world, for over the next three centuries the spectacular *Vasa* refuses to rot!

Who's responsible?

Ballast and bottoms! She's top-heavy.

Arrest the ship's captain!

That gust of wind tips the ship.

Uh-oh. No one covers the gun ports. Water gushes in through the double row of holes in the heeling ship.

What a wobbly ship! VASA is too heavy above the waterline and the ballast below is too light. That's downright unstable!

In the 1950s, amateur archaeologist Anders Franzen hunts through old documents and discovers VASA's story. The search is on. Aha! In August 1956, Franzen sees a piece of old oak wood in the jaws of his core sampler. This device that nibbles samples of seabed has just taken a bite out of VASA!

The wreck is 30 meters (100 feet) deep and is in such good shape that plans are made to pull it out of the water. Divers patch the damage done by 17th-century salvagers and replace thousands of rusty old bolts. Don't forget to cover the gun ports! On April 24, 1961, after five years of careful preparation, VASA is lifted to the surface with cables under her keel.

What? No rot?! Nasty wood-munching worms called Teridos navalis can't survive in the brackish (only slightly salty) sea near Stockholm. That's why wooden VASA is the best-preserved 17th-century warship in the world.

The 17th-century warship is emptied of water and floats for the first time in 333 years.

VASA's 64 cannons are recovered in 1664 and 1665 using the newly invented diving bell.

The remains of 25 skeletons hide in the wreck.

Experts carefully preserve the wreck and rebuild the damaged and destroyed parts, using the original timbers. Then the fantastic carvings, found in the mud, are reattached and VASA shows off her spectacular beauty once more.

Where's VASA today? See page 29.

Old Fish Tale

My ancient fossils are found in Europe and South America.

Of course, I'm not extinct! Now scientists wonder what other secrets hide in the sea.

 ere's a true and terrific tale of an ancient fish called the coelacanth (pronounced see-la-kanth) that swam the seas some 400 million years ago.

Scientists study ancient fossils of this super-scaly fish with its strange fringed tail and fins that look like lizard legs, and believe that the coelacanth has been extinct for over 70 million years.

Ha! What do the scientists know? They are dead wrong!

On December 22, 1938, the fishing boat NERINE pulls up its deep-sea nets at the mouth of South Africa's Chalumna River. An unknown, big, and scaly fish with very strange fins flops onto the deck—then stays alive for nearly four hours!

Down at the fishing wharf, NERINE's weird catch of the day is spotted by Marjorie Courtenay Latimer, head of a local museum. What is it? Latimer hasn't a clue. But she'll find out!

Pee-yooo! I must stop this fish from rotting. Only two places in town have enough ice to chill the fish, but neither the cold storage warehouse nor the hospital's mortuary (where dead people are kept cool before being buried) wants to store this stinky fish!

I'm having a rotten day!

My football−sized head hides a brain the size of a grape.

I can't survive in shallow water.

I can swim on my back and stand on my head.

I'm as long as an average nine−year−old child but weigh almost twice as much.

My eggs are grapefruit size.

If I swim too close to the surface, my light−reflecting eyes glow in the dark.

My skeleton is mostly cartilage (like human ears and noses). My spine is hollow and filled with oily fluid.

In a race against time, Latimer has no choice but to take the rotting fish to a taxidermist, who can preserve only its skin. Then she makes and mails a sketch to icthyologist (fish expert) James Leonard Brierly Smith, who is shocked to see a picture of an extinct coelacanth!

If there is one coelacanth in the sea, there have to be more! J.L.B. Smith sends posters to coastal fishing villages, offering a big reward for a fresh coelacanth. Nearly 14 years later, on December 20, 1952, a second one is finally caught at the Comoro Islands. Now scientists can study this ancient creature—inside and out.

AFRICA

Indian Ocean

Comoro Islands

East London
Indian Ocean

Since 1952, more coelacanths are caught in this spot, and many scientists think this is the fish's last hiding place on earth. Wrong! In 1998, a coelacanth is discovered in the waters of Indonesia, over 8,000 kilometers (5,000 miles) away.

The Wickedest City

Oooh arghh, 'tis the wickedest city on earth! In the late 17th century, Jamaica's Port Royal has a really rotten reputation, and no wonder. This Caribbean settlement is home to hundreds of pirates and buccaneers who spend their stolen gold on gambling, drinking, and making merry mischief.

But the pirate party ends on June 7, 1692, when a massive earthquake roars under the streets and two-thirds of the busy city suddenly slides into the sea. Shiver me timbers!

Now time stops for the sunken city, hiding on the harbor floor. It's trapped forever in a wet 17th-century time capsule.

Plunge in and take a peek into Port Royal's pirate past.

Yo-ho-ho and a bottle of rum! This tavern on Lime Street is full of bottles, beer tankards, and kegs.

The tools show that this shoemaker's shop is shared by a wood turner.

Ooops! Me potty slipped.

By thunder! Port Royal isn't just a pirate town, 'tis a busy business center for trading ships, sugar, and slaves. In 1692, it's the biggest, richest English settlement in the Americas.

Time stops for this pocket watch at 11:43 a.m.—the moment Port Royal sinks.

Blimey, me rum tasteth odde.

Lime Street

In 1692, Port Royal's population is over 6,500. The earthquake kills 2,000 people in minutes. Over the next 30 years, the city burns in a fire, then gets plastered with a hurricane and two more earthquakes. People take the hint and move across the bay to Kingston. Port Royal fades to a fishing village.

Lots of chamber pots sit in the ruins. In the days before flush toilets, city life was pretty stinky.

17

Under the Ice

Chill out with a super-cool story and discover an old 19th-century sailing ship, the *Breadalbane*, that hides under the ice in the Canadian Arctic.

On August 21, 1853, the *Breadalbane* is involved in a massive search for the missing explorer John Franklin. While the crew try to unload supplies, great slabs of ice shove the ship out to sea, then squeeze. Ouch! *Breadalbane* sinks in 15 minutes near Beechey Island, but the lucky crew scrambles over the ice to safety and hops on board another ship.

What happens next? Cuddle up to an ice cube and get in the mood for an icy Arctic adventure.

Do you know that the missing explorer John Franklin was looking for the Northwest Passage? Since the 16th century, Europeans have sought a northern route from the Atlantic to the Pacific—a faster way to get to the rich Orient—but by the 1800s everyone realizes that an Arctic route is too dangerous.

This is no time to get cold feet. Jump!

But the British navy keeps exploring the North and sends out their 58th expedition. In 1845, John Franklin and 129 men sail two ships—the EREBUS and the TERROR—into the Arctic. Then they disappear. Now lots of ships are looking for Franklin and the Northwest Passage too.

Look, I don't need a history lesson while I'm trying to save my life!

BREADALBANE is the northernmost shipwreck in the world.

In 1976, Dr. Joe MacInnis reads an old report that describes where BREADALBANE sinks—and the search is on! In 1980, from the deck of a Canadian icebreaker, the search team tows an underwater side-scan sonar device that emits sound waves and records what bounces back. The data goes up to a shipboard machine that prints black-and-white images of the sea floor.

Aha! Here's the BREADALBANE! Cameras are lowered down to see the ship and in 1983, after two years of bad ice conditions, diver Phil Nuytten is the first man in 130 years to walk BREADALBANE's decks.

NORTH POLE

NORTH MAGNETIC POLE

BEECHEY ISLAND

BREADALBANE SINKS HERE

NORTHWEST PASSAGE

ALASKA

CANADA

PACIFIC OCEAN

NORTHWEST PASSAGE

ATLANTIC OCEAN

The ship sinks a soccer-field's length under the ice.

FRANKLIN EXPEDITION

EREBUS AND TERROR SINK HERE

KING WILLIAM ISLAND

STARVATION COVE

All aboard! Shrimp, sea stars, anemones, and coral crowd onto the wooden wreck.

What happens to the Franklin Expedition?

An old document and a trail of bones and artifacts tell the story. For two years the ships are trapped in the ice near King William Island. In April 1848, 105 survivors quit the ships and slog south, dragging three life rafts loaded with curtain rods, cutlery, plates, prayer books, and even a writing desk.

Why do they drag a heavy desk over the ice? See page 30.

Brrrr. It's cold! For ten months of the year the ice is too thick to sail through. As for the other two months, shifting ice packs can blow in and sink a ship or trap it in a bay for years!

When the last 30 survivors reach a point now known as Starvation Cove, they link the known waters of the East and West, and discover the Northwest Passage. But no one lives to tell about it. (Robert McClure finds a route five years later.)

Black Smokers

Hot magma! Tall chimneys are growing right out of the rocks and they're belching a stinky toxic brew of super-hot mineral water, black smoke, and enough hydrogen sulfide chemicals to kill life as we know it in seconds. Within months, these black smokers grow as tall as a chimney on a two-story house!

If that isn't strange enough, all sorts of bizarre beasties seem to appear out of nowhere and crowd into one of the most poisonous places on the planet.

Scientists first see these weird wonders in 1977, while investigating an area of underwater volcanoes in the Pacific Ocean, and have since discovered several more sites in the Pacific and the Atlantic.

What's happening down in the deep dark sea? Hold your nose (that hydrogen sulfide chemical stinks like rotten eggs), dive down, and see.

The scientific name for a black smoker is "hydrothermal vent." Hydro means water, thermal is heat, and a vent is a small opening.

Wait a minute! Plants can't grow without sunlight, and it's blacker than black down here. So what do these creatures eat?

Plenty! Some of that hot toxic brew spewing out of the chimney is hydrogen sulfide. Billions of bacteria turn this chemical into a nourishing meal through a process called chemosynthesis. Bacteria feed the worms that feed the crabs that feed the octopus ...

Chemicals for breakfast. Yummy!

Whoopee! Dead bacteria for lunch!

Worms for dessert! Slurp.

Blast! Molten volcanic rock, or magma, explodes up to the seabed, crusts over quickly when it meets the near-freezing sea, then cracks under the weight of all that water pressing down on it. Sea water drains into the cracks, meets the still-hot magma below, and absorbs all sorts of minerals and chemicals.

Whoosh! The super-hot liquid finds an exit and blasts back up to the sea. Minerals in the gushing flow stick to the rim of the exit, forming a low chimney that quickly grows taller as more minerals pile on top.

Search for black smokers on the undersea cracks in the earth's crust, where a volcanic mountain ridge system, roughly 64,000 kilometers (40,000 miles) long, snakes around the globe.

Black smoker sites can be as small as your bedroom or as big as a tennis court.

The *Hunley* Mystery

BOOM! This explosion at sea in the American Civil War makes world history. The *H.L. Hunley* has just become the first submarine ever to sink an enemy ship.

On the moonlit night of February 17, 1864, in the waters near Charleston, South Carolina, U.S.A., this newly designed and built man-powered submarine rams the steam-powered sailing vessel *Housatonic* with its spearhead bomb. The bomb sticks into the enemy ship's hull, then the *Hunley* backs off to yank the detonating line. *Housatonic* burns and sinks in only three minutes.

But this important piece of war history ends in a mystery. For after the sub surfaces to signal its success to nearby Sullivan's Island, the *Hunley* with its eight-man crew disappears into the night without a trace, then hides for 131 years!

It's America's Civil War—a conflict between the northern (Union) and the southern (Confederate) states over the future of a united country. During the entire war (1861–1865), all southern ports are blockaded by northern ships, and anything trying to enter or leave the harbors is fired upon. But the southern port city Charleston fights back with a secret submarine.

Keep cranking that shaft! It turns the propeller and pushes us through the water at three knots. That's jogging speed.

Yikes! This attack mission is so risky that all the crew are volunteers. The HUNLEY sank twice in practice runs, and 13 out of the 17 former crew members were killed, including the sub's inventor, Horace L. Hunley. Each time the sub sinks, it's raised to the surface by salvage ships.

I hope Lieutenant Dixon has his lucky gold coin. We need all the help we can get!

Look over there! It must be that secret weapon that our spies warned us about. Uh-oh, our bullets bounce off it and our cannons can't point that low.

Ooof! Watch your elbows.

Don't get cranky, this 12-meter (40-foot) sub is tiny inside. It's made from a train's steam boiler with a diameter just a little bigger than a Hula Hoop.

Where's the HUNLEY hiding? The mystery is solved over a century later!

The National Underwater Marine Agency, headed by best-selling author Clive Cussler, hunts for the HUNLEY for 14 years. In 1995, their search ship's magnometer (a fancy metal detector) spots the iron sub under a layer of mud, just 9 meters (30 feet) under the sea.

The rusty wreck, lying in the Atlantic near Charleston's harbor, is lifted onto land in 2000. Scientists carefully empty the mud-filled sub, finding buttons, pocket knives, tobacco pipes, and more, as well as the bones of the brave eight-man crew.

An old story is told about a lucky gold coin given to Lieutenant George Dixon by his sweetheart, Queenie. (Dixon's the man at the front of the sub and the leader of the HUNLEY's historic combat mission.) The coin in Dixon's pocket stops a bullet and saves his life in the Civil War battle at Shiloh. Is the story true? A dented gold coin is found in the muddy sub next to Dixon's remains. Check out its inscription!

Shiloh
April 6th 1862
My life Preserver
G.E.D.

What sinks the sub? See page 30.

23

Spaceship Wreck

What's the strangest shipwreck in the sea? This cone-shaped "can" takes the prize. It's the *Liberty Bell 7*, an American spaceship that splashes down into the Atlantic Ocean on July 21, 1961, after arching 190 kilometers (118 miles) above the earth.

Uh-oh, here comes the shipwreck bit. While waiting to be plucked from the sea by a recovery helicopter, *Liberty Bell 7*'s special explosive side hatch (astronaut exit) blows off ahead of schedule. The capsule fills up with sea water and sinks to the deep ocean floor, becoming America's only space capsule ever lost at sea.

Now put on your space helmet and gravity boots and read all about this astronomical spaceship wreck!

LIBERTY BELL 7 is a Mercury spacecraft, launched with a Redstone rocket from Cape Canaveral, Florida. It is designed and built by NASA (National Aeronautics and Space Administration). The space flight lasts 15 minutes 37 seconds.

Splashdown!
Astronaut Gus Grissom climbs out of the hatch and falls into the sea. He has just become the third human ever to return from space.

Yikes! The man in a can has a leak in his spacesuit and nearly drowns.

Don't worry, Gus is saved before he sinks.

Did you know that ASTRONAUT means "star sailor"?

Wow! Does NAUGHTYNAUT mean "bad sailor"?

Finding LIBERTY BELL 7 won't be easy. Its hiding place is even deeper than the famous shipwreck TITANIC—and that's deep! The spacecraft sits some 5 kilometers (3 miles) down on the sea floor.

It's a shrimp of a shipwreck! The space capsule will fit inside a small bathroom.

In April 1999, shipwreck specialist Curt Newport searches for this important piece of U.S. space history. Using the latest technology, Curt and his deep-sea salvage team map the ups and downs of the seabed with sonar, then take a closer look at the first of 88 interesting-looking lumps with an ROV (Remotely Operated Vehicle). Amazingly, the ROV spots the lost capsule on its very first dive.

Astronomical! The spaceship wreck is sitting upright and looks almost ready for liftoff! The painted words "LIBERTY BELL 7" and "United States" are easy to read.

On July 20, 1999, the world's strangest shipwreck is pulled out of the sea and sees the sky for the first time in 38 years.

The spacecraft is taken ashore, carefully disassembled, cleaned, then restored. Phew! What a lot of work. LIBERTY BELL 7 has some 26,000 parts!

Where is LIBERTY BELL 7 today? See page 29.

Getting Down!

Can you hold your breath for 30 seconds? A minute? However long, it's easy to see that getting down deep underwater is a big problem for us air-breathing humans.

But that doesn't stop us! Over the centuries, people plunge down deeper and deeper in search of sponges, pearls, sunken treasure wrecks, and more!

How do we do it? Dive in and see!

Plunge into the past and become a deep-diving expert.

START

Getting down 500 meters (1,640 feet) is no problem in this modern pressure suit. Without it, the diver will be crushed!

SWIM AHEAD 1 SPACE

In 1960, August Piccard's bathyscaphe TRIESTE is the first craft to get humans down to the deepest of the deep, at 10,913 meters (35,813 feet).

Nitrogen strikes again! You dive 30 meters (100 feet) below sea level and start acting really silly and sloppy. Divers call it "raptures of the deep."

At 91 meters (300 feet), the gas can kill you.

I can breathe underwater and swim as free as a fish.

CONGRATULATIONS! You live in very exciting times. Deep-sea explorers discover hidden secrets every year!

FINISH

Climb into a submersible. These super-strong mini-submarines are designed to explore the deep ocean floor with lights, cameras, and robot arms, all operated by their two- or three-person crews.

Goodbye air hoses! In 1943, Jacques-Yves Cousteau and Emile Gagnan invent the modern scuba (Self-Contained Underwater Breathing Apparatus).

From World War I in 1914 to the present day, submarines have developed into deadly weapons of war.

Man the torpedoes!

GO BACK 7 SPACES

I can dive down 4,400 meters (14,500 feet).

Most underwater work is done today with an ROV. Stay on board your ship and drop the Remotely Operated Vehicle to the sea floor. Through a long cable, you can tell it where to go and what to pick up.

"I can hold my breath for nearly three minutes!"

MISS A TURN

People dive for pearls over 4,300 years ago. In 2300 BCE, the Chinese book SHU KING complains of a "string of pearls not quite round."

Here's some ancient history! Herodotus writes in 500 BCE about Syllis, a Greek sailor who uses a hollow reed snorkel to sneak up on enemy Persian ships and cut their mooring lines.

SWIM AHEAD 1 SPACE

The first successful diving bells are lowered into the water around the 17th century. Now divers can swim inside for a breath of trapped air. Is the air running low? More air, stored in sealed barrels, is emptied inside the bell.

Gasp! The man in this 1797 diving suit can't breathe. His hose leads to a container of air that quickly runs out.

MISS A TURN

What do you get when you cross a diving bell with a submarine? How about this diving barrel built by John Lethbridge in 1715?

Yippee! I can reach this wreck 18 meters (60 feet) deep.

In 1776, America's TURTLE is the first submarine to attack a ship. Unfortunately, it can't screw through the English ship's copper bottom to attach the explosives.

You can't swim. GO BACK TO START

It all comes together in 1837 when Augustus Siebe invents a waterproof suit with a tightly sealed metal helmet. The ship above pumps down air through a supply hose.

I can reach 30 meters (100 feet) deep and stay as long as I need to.

Uh-oh. In the 1840s, divers double up in pain. The problem is pressure. Every 10 meters (33 feet) of water weighs the same as the earth's atmosphere, which presses down on you at one kilogram per square centimeter (14.7 pounds per square inch).

ROLL AGAIN

Quick! Get into the decompression chamber! MISS A TURN

ROLL AGAIN

You are deep-sea pressurized then slowly returned to normal, giving those nitrogen bubbles time to pass through to your lungs. Now breathe out!

Ow! You have the bends, or decompression sickness.

When you return to the surface, slow down! Those bubbles need time to pop back into your lungs. If you're too quick, the bubbles stay put and you bend over in pain.

When you dive down just a few atmospheres deep, the extra pressure forces the nitrogen from your lungs (78% of air is nitrogen) into your blood.

GO BACK 1 SPACE

Get Serious!

This page has lots of salty secrets!

Start your shipwreck search with research. Read history books, old documents, maps, and reports found in library archives and government records. Listen to local fishermen. Have their nets pulled up broken pottery pieces or snagged on something big beneath the sea?

Help! That wooden wheel looked perfect under the sea, but on dry land it quickly shrinks and splits. Out of the water, that metal porthole crumbles into a bucket of rust and that beautiful bronze cannon belches green powder blotches.

Experts know that sea-soaked artifacts quickly decay after they are pulled up to the surface. The water in the soaking-wet wood must be slowly replaced with polyethylene glycol to stop the wood from self-destructing as it dries. Metals must be treated with electrolysis and chemical baths. This takes time: a wooden wheel needs a year-long bath (maybe longer), and a whole ship like VASA takes a 17-year shower!

If your fishing net pulls up a super ship bit, keep it wet in a tub of fresh water. The artifact will be safe from rot, rust, or crumble while you and your parents research the best way to preserve it. Get expert advice at your local museum, or search the library and the Internet.

Ooops! Before you swim off with that sunken ship's bell, you should check to see if the wreck is protected by local or federal laws. If the wreck lies close to shore, it probably is. This means that the wreck can't be wrecked by souvenir hunters but must stay intact for future generations to see and study.

How many shipwrecks hide in the sea? There must be thousands!

If you find a wreck in international waters, you are free to take all the treasure and artifacts that you can get.

An artifact is a man-made object like a ship's bell, a sailor's shoe, or an old glass bottle. Artifacts are not nearly as valuable as treasure, but they show us how people lived in the past.

Take a closer look at some of the discoveries in this book.

MUSEUM

Treasure Hunt
(pages 6–7)

Pearls are everywhere—in stores, museums, and maybe your mother's jewelry box.

Vung Tao's ceramic cargo is in the hands of private collectors.

Search for Central America's rare gold coins in museums' numismatic collections as well as traveling numismatic exhibits. Numiswhat? *Numismatic* means money.

Sunken Spanish treasure shines in many museums. Don't miss some of the *Atocha*'s fantastic fortune at the Mel Fisher Museum in Key West, Florida, U.S.A.

Girona's gold jewelry now glitters at the Ulster Museum in Belfast, Northern Ireland.

Where's *Whydah*'s pirate plunder? Visit Expedition *Whydah* Sea Lab & Learning Center in Provincetown, Massachusetts, U.S.A.

Ancient Sea Creatures
(pages 8–9)

See Burgess Shale fossils at the Smithsonian Institution's National Museum of Natural History in Washington, DC, U.S.A., or get ready for an all-day hike in Yoho National Park, British Columbia, Canada, for a guided tour of this ancient seashore at Walcott's Quarry.

Long-lost Lighthouse
(pages 10–11)

Find some of Pharos's long-lost-lighthouse ruins at the Open Air Museum in Alexandria, Egypt, then stand tall at Fort Qait Bey, built over the site of the seventh wonder of the ancient world.

Wobbly Warship
(pages 12–13)

Visit *Vasa*. The whole ship is high and dry in the *Vasa* Museum, Stockholm, Sweden.

Old Fish Tale
(pages 14–15)

A cast of Marjorie Latimer's original coelacanth is at the East London Museum, South Africa. Larger museums and aquariums often have coelacanth displays much closer to home, but don't expect to see the real fish: they usually hide in research rooms, protected and preserved in alcohol.

The Wickedest City
(pages 16–17)

Oooh arghh! Awesome artifacts, salvaged from the sunken 17th-century city, can be found at the Port Royal Archaeological and Historical Museum in Port Royal, Jamaica.

Under the Ice
(pages 18–19)

Want to get up close to the northernmost shipwreck in the world? Save your pennies (you'll need LOTS), climb into a sightseeing submersible, and dive down to the *Breadalbane* under Canada's freezing Northwest Passage. Brrr.

Black Smokers
(pages 20–21)

Are you a marine scientist? No? Then you won't be visiting a real deep-sea vent site any time soon. But you can see a life-size display, such as the one at the American Museum of Natural History, New York City, NY, U.S.A. Check your nearest natural history museum or aquarium.

The *Hunley* Mystery
(pages 22–23)

Where's the *Hunley* hiding? Find the Civil War sub at the Warren Lasch Conservation Center in Charleston, South Carolina, U.S.A. Don't forget to pay your respects to the *Hunley*'s brave crew, buried in Charleston's Magnolia Cemetery.

Spaceship Wreck
(pages 24–25)

If your orbit takes you near Kansas, U.S.A., then drop into the Kansas Cosmosphere and Space Center to see *Liberty Bell 7*. Astronomical!

Curious?

The Wickedest City
(pages 16–17)

These objects don't belong in the 17th century!

Under the Ice
(pages 18–19)

Why do they drag a heavy writing desk over the ice?

Why do the last Franklin Expedition survivors drag heavy dishes, curtain rods, a big desk, and more over the ice? Are they crazy? Possibly.

In 1981, anthropologist Owen Beattie digs up the graves of three crew members buried on Beechey Island to examine their frozen, perfectly preserved bodies. One man has far too much of the metal lead in his body—100 times the normal amount! Lead poisoning alters how you think, and you can make some very strange decisions!

But where does the lead come from? Food tins! Rusty cans found at the expedition's campsites are sealed with lead solder. The lead leaches into the food and slowly poisons the men every time they make a meal from one of the expedition's 8,000 cans. (Relax, modern cans have no lead.)

The *Hunley* Mystery
(pages 22–23)

What sinks the sub?

Did you see part of a water tank in the sub's cut-away picture? Experts wonder if the fault lies here. Sea water is pumped into or out of the *Hunley*'s two open-topped tanks. The weight of the sea water controls how high or low the sub sits in the sea.

But these water tanks can easily overflow and spill inside the sub. Did someone forget to check the water levels, or was there a problem with the valves that let sea water enter or leave through the sub's wall? If an overflowing water tank can't be emptied, the *Hunley* becomes far too heavy to float back up to the sea surface. This is how the *Hunley* sank for the second time, on October 15, 1863, killing all eight crew members, including the sub's inventor, Horace L. Hunley.

Treasure Hunt
(pages 6–7)

It's the way through the maze and the location of 15 delicious fish!

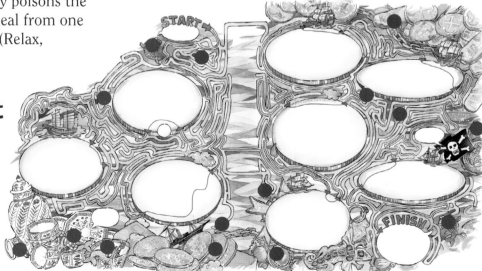

30

L·I·B·R·A·R·Y

Prehistory

Aliki. FOSSILS TELL OF LONG AGO. New York: Harper Trophy, 1990. (Age Level 4–8)

Levy, Elizabeth. WHO ARE YOU CALLING A WOOLLY MAMMOTH?: PREHISTORIC AMERICA. America's Horrible Histories Series. New York: Scholastic, 1999. (Age Level 9–11)

Trueit, Trudi Strain. FOSSILS. New York: Franklin Watts, 2003. (Age Level 10–12)

Lighthouses

Gibbons, Gail. BEACONS OF LIGHT: LIGHTHOUSES. New York: William Morrow, 1990. (Age Level 4–8)

Guiberson, Brenda Z. LIGHT-HOUSES: WATCHERS AT SEA. New York: Henry Holt, 1995. (Age Level 9–12)

Pirates

Gibbons, Gail. PIRATES: ROBBERS OF THE HIGH SEAS. New York: Little, Brown, 1999. (Age Level 4–7)

Marrin, Albert. TERROR OF THE SPANISH MAIN: SIR HENRY MORGAN AND HIS BUCCANEERS. New York: Penguin Putnam Books for Young Readers, 1999. (Age Level 12 and up)

Steele, Philip. PIRATES. Boston: Houghton Mifflin, 1997. (Age Level 8–12)

The Franklin Expedition

Beattie, Owen, and John Geiger. BURIED IN ICE. Time Quest Books. New York: Scholastic, 1992. (Age Level 8–12)

Volcanoes

Lauber, Patricia. VOLCANO: THE ERUPTION AND HEALING OF MOUNT ST. HELENS. New York: Simon & Schuster, 1999. (Age Level 9–12)

Simon, Seymour. DANGER! VOLCANOES. Seemore Readers. New York: SeaStar Books, 2002. (Age Level 4–8)

Van, Susanna Rose. EYEWITNESS: VOLCANO & EARTHQUAKE. Eyewitness Books. New York: DK Publishing, 2000. (Age Level 9–12)

The *Hunley*

Jerome, Kate Boehm. CIVIL WAR SUB: THE MYSTERY OF THE *HUNLEY*, Vol. 3. All Aboard Reading Series. New York: Grosset & Dunlap, 2002. (Age Level 9–12)

Space

Berger, Melvin, and Gilda Berger. CAN YOU HEAR A SHOUT IN SPACE?: QUESTIONS AND ANSWERS ABOUT SPACE EXPLORATION. Question and Answer Series. New York: Scholastic, 2000. (Age Level 9–12)

Bredeson, Carmen. GUS GRISSOM: A SPACE BIOGRAPHY. Countdown to Space Series. Springfield: Enslow Publishers, 1998. (Age Level 10–14)

Ride, Sally, and Susan Okie. TO SPACE AND BACK. New York: William Morrow, 1986. (Age Level 7–11)

Diving

Bankston, John. JACQUES-YVES COUSTEAU: HIS STORY UNDER THE SEA. Hockessin, DE: Mitchell Lane Publishers, 2002. (Age Level 12 and up)

Berger, Melvin. DIVE!: A BOOK OF DEEP SEA CREATURES. Hello Reader! Science Series. New York: Scholastic, 2000. (Age Level 5–7)

Hook, Sue Vander. DEEP DIVING ADVENTURES. Dangerous Adventures Series. Mankato, MN: Capstone Press, 2000. (Age Level 8–12)

Index

Acknowledgments

Thanks to Sheryl Shapiro of Annick Press for her encouragement and friendly professionalism, and to my son Tom Morgan for kid-testing all the information. Thank you to the Toronto Public Library, Friends of the *Hunley*, NASA, the Nautical Archaeology Program – Texas A & M University, the Center for Alexandrian Studies, *Vasa* Museum, and the Smithsonian Institution. Any errors or omissions are of course entirely my own.